Page Not Found

Why most business websites fail
and how to help ensure yours doesn't.

Jonathan Clark

Founder of Diginovas

ISBN 978-1-387-14796-0

For all the people crazy enough to risk public humiliation, financial loss, and their sanity by starting a business.

Contents

Introduction

First, a little perspective.

On a cold, crisp autumn morning not too long ago, I was discussing a new project with a business owner. In business since 1989, his company had *never* had a web presence.

He handed me a large three-ring binder with a stylish, corporate-looking cover. Inside was his brand's story, his company's certifications, and descriptions of projects his company had completed.

Looking down at the binder, he said, *"I've been in business for more than two decades, but when I meet with a potential client, they ask for my website. And because I don't have one, it's like my business doesn't exist."*

When I began my design career in 2001, most businesses had no web presence.

In fact, the most significant challenge I faced in those days was convincing a business owner that they *needed* a website.

Consider that at that time, for many businesses, the primary advertising vehicle was an ad in the yellow pages of the local phone book. And it wasn't uncommon to spend thousands of dollars each month for those ads!

Before Google, search engines weren't the sophisticated, algorithm-driven software that powers advanced search today. They were more like static directories.

Indeed, your business was more likely to be found in your yellow page ad than online.

Around 2009, my yellow page rep offered ad rates that were lower than the previous year for the first time — a most telling sign. It seemed like the paradigm had begun to shift in how people searched for products and services from print to online.

Back in 2001, the top search engine was *Yahoo!*, the average computer screen resolution was a mere eight hundred pixels wide (HD is 1920 pixels), and the primary method of browsing websites was on a desktop computer using Internet Explorer — using a 56k dial-up connection!

Oh, and the iPhone was still six years away from changing the world.

To say that things have changed since the time I started designing websites is a gross understatement.

How websites fail.

To understand what failure looks like for a business website, we should begin with the objectives and goals of a site. Unfortunately, proper planning — a vital step — is left out of the process for many business websites.

It doesn't take much digging to discern the amount of planning that went into any given website — usually no further than the home page to view the title and description, which in many cases are merely the name of the site followed by "Home."

Effective websites are designed with a content-first approach and supported by a manageable and realistic governance plan that align with specific objectives and goals.

What was true in 2001 remains true today: Users come for content. And the simple reason most websites fail to engage their target audience is the lack of relevant content.

The idea that "content is king" shouldn't be a revelation to most people. But the proliferation of pre-built website templates and themes have, in many ways, created a false sense of the correct level of difficulty involved in modern website development.

Building a website is not unlike building a house.

You begin with a plan, a project manager assembles a team, the house is constructed, then inspected, and *voila*! You have a house.

But instead of starting from scratch, imagine what would happen if the construction company began with a pre-constructed house and then set out to customize it to your idea of what it should look like and how it should function?

It's likely that there would be a lot of sacrifices and compromises to stay within budget and on schedule.

Something like this scenario plays out in website development all the time.

And it's often a cost-driven strategy employed by young design companies, which all too often amount to nothing more than someone with a laptop, working from the basement in their parent's house.

Like building a house, several distinct disciplines need to be engaged if the website is going to have a chance at success.

While the model varies from company to company, the lineup for a web development team looks something like this:

Business Strategist / Marketing Specialist

The person who works with the client to determine business needs, goals, objectives, search strategy, social media, project budget, and schedule. This person typically creates the initial sitemap.

Content Developer

On small projects, this may be one person. A team of specialized writers may be required on larger projects. Collectively, this team writes the words, sources the images, and works with the front-end designers to create the appropriate language to complete calls-to-action, form buttons, and any other language, including search engine optimization.

Designers / Programmers

There are typically two types of web developers: front-end and back-end. Simply put, front-end people make the site look good (designers) and back-end people make the site work.

Testers

Testers are the people who review the site before launch and ensure the website performs as expected.

They may employ specialty browsers or tools to emulate the different ways users will experience their website: from High-Definition TVs to the smallest smartphone.

In many cases, testers also check the search engine optimization information to ensure search engines index pages correctly and display the correct information on search results pages.

The launch is just the beginning.

While the launch of a new (or redesigned) website is typically a significant event, it's just another notch on the timeline of the life of a site. Indeed, the work has just begun.

It's never been easier to create a website, **but it's not so easy to create an effective website** — one that delivers on its goals and objectives.

And this is where many businesses make their second mistake: lacking a governance plan for managing the website after it's launched.

Without proper care and attention, it's unlikely your website will reach your goals. And for most sites, that begins with traffic. But not just any traffic — traffic from *your* target market.

This is where your content marketing plan kicks in and works in concert with your search engine strategy.

I've written this book with the small business owner or startup in mind, and I've intentionally left out technical terms and limited the use of acronyms that might be distracting.

However, there are a few terms that may be unfamiliar to many readers, so here's a quick primer.

Web Server: A computer that stores webserver software and a website's component files, documents, and images. It delivers content or services to end users over the Internet.

Server Hosting: This refers to the outsourcing of an organization's web server placement and platform to a third-party provider who usually operates and manages large data centers with dozens, hundreds, or thousands of hosted servers. It's an economical way for organizations to eliminate the overhead logistics associated with operating a server or data center.

Domain Name: An Internet resource name that is universally understood by Web servers and online organizations and provides all pertinent destination information. Domain names have two parts that are separated by a dot, such as example.com.

Content Marketing: The use of digital or print content to drive audience engagement. Some of the most common forms of content including online blog posts, white papers, e-books, or videos that can be embedded in Facebook or Twitter posts or posted on other social media platforms.

Search Engine Rank: This refers to the position a Web page holds in the results for a specific query. There may be many pages of results depending on the query, so the search rank refers to the results page on which a given Web page appears as well as its position on that page.

Search Engine Optimization (SEO): SEO often involves the creation and organization of keyword-rich content and optimized coding to increase traffic to a website by increasing its search engine rank.

IT Management: This is the process whereby all resources related to information technology are managed according to an organization's priorities and needs. This includes tangible resources like networking hardware, computers and people, and intangible resources like software and data.

Social Media: This is a catch-all term for a variety of internet applications that allow users to create content and interact with each other. The term is more strongly identified with sites like Twitter, Facebook, LinkedIn, and Instagram.

Content Management System: An interface that allows users to create, edit and publish content to a website from anywhere and at any time.

Copy: Text used in the content of a website or other marketing materials.

Meta Tag: An element that provides information about the metadata of a web page that is used by web services and search engines but is not visible to the end-user without viewing the page source code.

Covering the Basics

CHAPTER ONE

When I started my first web design business in 2002, it took someone with a technical understanding of the Internet to launch even the simplest of websites.

Today, it doesn't take much to get a website up and running. For many startups, online services like Weebly, Wix, or Squarespace can provide an inexpensive (and relatively simple) on-ramp to a business website.

Getting your new business online is undoubtedly easier than ever before.

But it's important to understand that for most every website, there are three essential elements: domain name, hosting, and the content management system.

Domain Name

This is your web address [www.mywebsite.com] and once configured, it directs web traffic to the server hosting your website. There's a reason this is the first item I address — it is arguably the most critical piece of any site.

Buying a domain name is not an everyday activity for most people, and a standard mistake I've encountered is the lack of attention paid to the domain name account.

Business owners often relegate the upkeep of the domain to an assistant or a bookkeeper who, in many cases, files the information away and loses the credentials (login information). Often, a domain fails to get renewed, making the website unavailable, and in extreme cases, forfeiting ownership.

Hosting

Every website needs to be hosted on an Internet-connected server. While it is technically possible to host your site on a personal computer, it's not a great idea. There's typically a fee associated with hosting, but for many who use a website builder service (e.g., Wix, Weebly, etc.), hosting charges are usually included in the monthly fee.

Content Management System (CMS)

Most websites today make use of a content management system. Think of this as the website platform.

The most popular of these is WordPress. In fact, approximately thirty percent of all websites are powered by WordPress, according to W3 Techs.

The number of CMS options today is vast, and costs range from free to hundreds of thousands of dollars.

When it comes to choosing a CMS, there are many considerations, but there are two critical elements.

First, the CMS should fit the business objective of the website. So, if your objective is to sell products online, you should use a CMS built for e-commerce — not a blogging CMS that's been hacked or modified for e-commerce.

Second, the person who will be managing the site should have the requisite technical skills for the chosen CMS.

Make it easy to use.

With the proliferation of devices that connect to the Internet today, it's more important than ever to take into consideration how end-users will view and use your website.

A responsively-designed website that works as well (and looks as good), on an HD monitor as it does on a smartphone display — and everything in between — is where you should begin.

User-centered design is at the core of most effective websites and includes:

- clear objectives
- simple, user-friendly navigation
- concise, well-written language
- a plan of what content gets displayed based according to screen size
- incorporating unambiguous, strong calls to action (elements with eye-catching graphics, writing, and buttons that link to a specific action) throughout the site

While the user-centered design method is the norm for most web development firms today, implementing this strategy can be challenging (but not entirely impossible), when using a do-it-yourself service.

Don't let it gather dust.

For many businesses, the launch of a new website signals the completion of the project — and that's where it often ends, which is evident by the number of sites whose first and only blog article reads, "*Hello world! This is your first blog post.*"

Many factors go into proper Search Engine Optimization (SEO) of which the most important is relevant and timely content. (We'll cover SEO in more detail in Chapter Four.)

In fact, many marketers believe that Google and other search engines now value quality and authoritative content over traditional SEO.

Content marketing can be one of the most effective (and inexpensive) ways to stay in front of your audience.

Once published, blog articles, news articles, and videos can be distributed through social media channels, email marketing, and RSS (Really Simple Syndication) to extend the reach of your website.

I cannot stress enough the value of a good website content management plan.

What gets measured gets done. Measuring the effectiveness of a website should be an integral part of any governance plan.

Sure, your testing may have gone smoothly before the launch. But now you need to know if everything is working as hoped in a real-world environment.

While most CMS platforms have built-in analytics of some form, Google Analytics is where many web marketers turn to understand better and analyze how their website is performing.

Today, websites vary from the simple, one-page brochures to complex, cloud-based sites integrated with dissimilar software.

And clearly, there are many other factors and details for consideration within the web development process than noted here.

But, no matter what type of site your business requires, it's likely to be the first interaction with prospects — and the first opportunity to distinguish your business from your competitors.

Make sure you get these basics covered, so your website is available and ready for all those first impressions.

Content-First Design

CHAPTER TWO

The secret to a great website is great content.

There are over a billion websites in existence today, up from about 600 million in 2013.

And Google processes over 40,000 search queries every second, which translates to more than 3.5 billion searches per day.

The Internet is a crowded place.

To make sure your website stands out, you'll need more than a trendy design, a fancy logo, and pretty pictures.

Capturing the attention of your audience is exceedingly challenging in today's digital universe, especially when most web users spend fewer than fifteen seconds on a web page.

You'll need great content.

The dirty little secret of web design is that users come for content, not design. Content is the most critical element in web design.

A site with a simple design and quality content performs exponentially better in usability tests than a fancy layout with subpar copy.

But the proliferation of cheap, easy-to-install themes has contributed to the myth that content is a secondary consideration.

Indeed, even many experienced designers create their wireframes and mockups with "lorem ipsum" filler text.

While this may be more expedient, it relegates content to the role of a cheap commodity. And the design, while aesthetically pleasing, is in many cases, practically useless.

Stuffing a theme may or may not work.

More than a quarter of all websites on the Internet use some form of WordPress. It takes little effort, technical skills — or money — to launch a new WordPress website. *Today*.

And there are hundreds of attractive WordPress themes available, many of which have one thing in common: Photos are the main design component.

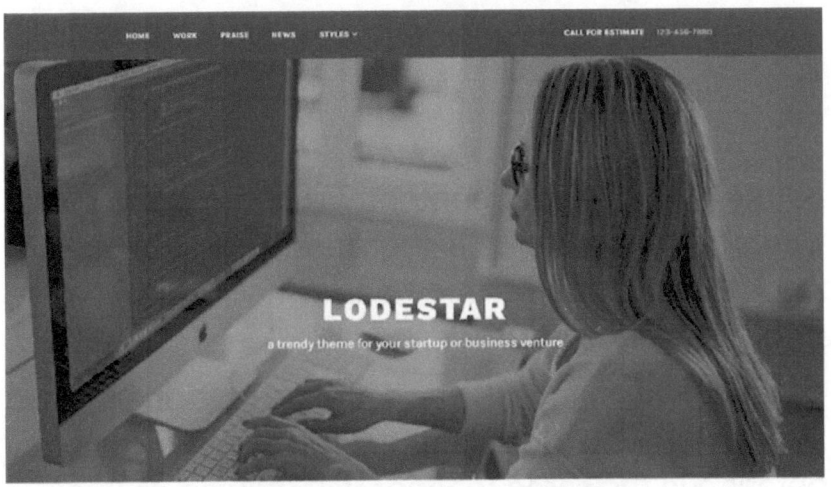

A common WordPress theme design.

But what happens to the design when you replace those stock images with your own? In many cases, the theme designer chose images that match the color palette of the design. And in almost all cases, you'll be letting the design drive the content, not the other way around.

Which often translates into ill-fitting images, awkward white spaces, and the opportunity for filler text to go terribly wrong.

And the chances your content will fit the same space as the placeholders in a theme are slim. In fact, in most cases, design restructuring is necessary to give some semblance of order.

Consider that many of these theme designers have day jobs at web design agencies and they're likely operating in the same manner with paying clients.

Why? Because sales execs and project managers often urge designers to deliver designs, wireframes, and mockups as quickly as possible to show impatient clients. Unfortunately, spending time on content slows down the completion of these deliverables.

The content-first strategy.

In an ideal situation, a content development specialist is one of the first people with whom you would consult; which doesn't happen nearly as much as it should, even with so-called professional web design companies.

Writing for the web, or for that matter, any medium takes knowledge and experience. Few web designers are writers and relying on them to write your web copy should be a scary proposition.

Beyond the standard "About Us" and "Services," a website is full of interfaces that need proper attention if you expect anyone to use it and get anything from it, much less provide a return on your investment.

If your site requires data input, for example, there are calls-to-action, button text, and labels that if sloppily written, reduce your site's efficacy.

Begin your content development with a purpose: What does this site need to do for you? Then create your content around that purpose and goals.

Take an inventory of everything that needs to be included to fulfill the site's purpose, then determine how that content will be structured as pages and how each page relates to each other.

What is your brand promise? How exactly do you want to communicate that promise to your website visitors?

Be mindful that as your site's content is being developed, you'll likely make many updates, especially after its launch.

An important aspect of website design that seems lost with many business owners is that a website is never finished.

To maximize your site's effectiveness, you'll want to keep adding and removing content, making revisions, adding new elements — and that's okay.

Great content helps people find your website.

One of the most critical factors in your site's search engine ranking is quality content. In fact, content is one of Google's most important ranking factors according to Andrey Lipattsev, a Search Quality Senior Strategist at Google.

Websites with rich, relevant subject information are the type of sites that find their way at the top of the search engine results pages. Get your content right, and you've created a solid foundation from which to build your search engine optimization efforts.

While a lot of importance is given to keyword placement, writing for your audience — and in the correct language — should be the most critical consideration.

Your site's content should focus on the interest of your visitors, address the question of what's in it for them, and help solve their problem.

If you want people to find your web pages for a specific word or phrase searches, it's always a good idea to include those words in your copy, headings, and page titles. Though how many keywords you should use is a hotly debated topic.

The best practice is to write for people, not for search engines by just stuffing a lot of keywords and phrases into your content. Your visitors will notice the difference.

Paul Boag has been building websites since 1994 and has written numerous articles and books on web design.

In one of his pieces on content strategy, he remarked, *"After 20 years building websites for clients, I'm still amazed at how completely clients underestimate the work involved in creating content for their website. I'm also gobsmacked every time a client happily pays for design and development, but won't spend a penny on content creation."*

You can choose to put in the effort required to create great content on the front side and build a website that engages your audience.

Or choose to take the seemingly easy path with pre-built themes and poor content. The latter will likely result in a website, but its efficacy may be questionable.

How Internet Traffic Works

CHAPTER THREE

It's not sexy, but it's essential to understand.

Before smartphones and the Internet, most everyone had a landline phone that was used for one purpose — to talk to other people. And if you wanted to call someone, you needed their phone number.

Because we're talking about basic telephones, there was no such thing as built-in directories that could be used to search or browse phone numbers. So, unless you had an exceptional memory, you most likely needed a phone book to find the number of a neighbor or business.

Consider for a moment what your world would look like if you had to remember (or look up the number) for your favorite website.

Perhaps a friend suggests a new website: 31.13.71.36.

While that address is relatively short, it's still more difficult to remember than Facebook.com.

The wonder of what we call, "DNS" is that it is the system that makes it possible for the Internet to know where to send traffic when you type a web address into a browser. It's the Internet's address book, and if your website's DNS isn't correctly configured, it can seriously ruin your day.

The domain name system.

The Domain Name System was created initially to support the growth of email in the early days of the ARPANET, what we refer to now as the Internet.

As technology evolved, this new naming system was developed to translate website names into computer addresses, or Internet Protocol (IP) addresses. The beauty of this system is that it makes it easy to move your website from server to server without having to notify everyone your site was relocated.

For instance, if Google decided to move its website to a different computer server, you needn't worry about it. Their engineers would update the DNS record to the new address, and you would still be able to view their website when you enter Google.com in the address bar of your browser.

There are many types of DNS records that work to direct traffic for your domain, but for this chapter (and to stay out of the tech weeds), we'll stick with just three: A, MX, and NS.

Why DNS is essential to your website — and your business.

As you might sense, it's essential to get your DNS records correctly configured if you want your website to work correctly.

But DNS also directs your email, so it's equally important to make sure your IT managers know what they're doing. You may never need to configure your DNS, but it's good to know the basics.

Address Record (A)

The A record tells the Internet on which server to find your website. To configure this, one would simply set the A record to the IP address of the server on which the site resides.

Mail Exchange Records (MX)

Like the A record, the MX record also directs traffic, but this record directs your email traffic.

If your website hosting provider provides your email service, it's likely that you won't need to change the MX record.

But if your organization is using a third-party email provider like Office 365 or G Suite (Gmail), the address will be different and require updating.

Name Server (NS)

The NS record tells the Internet where all your DNS records are stored.

You can choose to host your DNS records with your domain name registrar (think: GoDaddy), a DNS hosting provider, or your website hosting provider.

To simplify the DNS process, many hosting providers will recommend their customers store their DNS records on the website server.

While this may be simple and expedient, it's not always the best solution. Why? If your hosting provider goes offline, not only does your website go down, but so does your email.

Unfortunately, many business owners usually find this out the hard way.

And because website hosting, domain name registration, and email service have become somewhat commoditized over the past decade, it's often the case that business owners select the cheapest providers.

Until something goes wrong.

And if it can, it will — eventually.

DNS best practices.

Most IT professionals are likely to recommend hosting DNS records with the most reliable provider, which might be the domain name registrar or a reputable DNS hosting company. But it's unlikely to be your website hosting provider.

Consider that website hosting is rarely 100% reliable. And as I said before, if your website goes down and your DNS is hosted there, your email goes down with it, no matter what email service you happen to be using.

And for most organizations, email continues to be a vital communication tool — both internally and externally — which is why it's in the best interest of your businesses to use a dedicated email service.

Yes, most website hosting platforms include email service (typically for free or a small fee), but it's not usually the smartest choice.

First, you'll eventually run into storage issues. Website hosting is for hosting websites, not email, which means that your emails are using storage space that should be reserved for your website files, not email attachments.

And because email service is typically a secondary consideration with most website hosting providers, the interface, functionality, security, and support are often less than stellar.

Moreover, with a dedicated email provider like G Suite or Office 365, you get tons of extras like cloud storage, office productivity apps, and mobile email apps.

Lastly, it can lock you into your website provider. Migrating a website, while not the easiest chore, is a walk in the park compared to migrating email accounts.

There are many exceptions to these rules, but the importance of getting your DNS records configured correctly cannot be overstated.

And it's a conversation that should take place in the planning stages of your website with an experienced and trusted IT professional rather than after the site is live, or worse — just left to chance.

Make Sure Your Site Gets Found

CHAPTER FOUR

The basic elements of Search Engine Optimization.

For many small businesses and startups, the process of getting your website listed in search engines is likely to be as big of a mystery as Kanye West's success.

Where do you begin? Is it something you can do by yourself? Should you pay an expert, and if so, how much?

And unfortunately, the many myths surrounding Search Engine Optimization [SEO] often lead the do-it-yourself types down paths that end in disappointment and frustration.

Search optimization and marketing is a $65 billion-a-year industry, and it's estimated to surpass $79 billion by 2020. There's a reason for this: Quality SEO takes work, time, and most importantly, it requires an intimate knowledge of how search engines work.

While many factors determine how well a site ranks in any given search engine, there are a few basics that most anyone can understand and implement into their website.

But first, a little primer on what search engines are and how they work.

Search engines use software — sometimes called crawlers, bots, or spiders — to go from one website to another through hyperlinks. They take the information from each of those websites they've crawled and catalog it into their databases which later, can be recalled providing the appropriate result in response to the search query of a user.

One of the primary signals for search engines is link popularity, which is to say, the number of other websites that link to a website. A site with many inbound links from quality websites is one of the critical metrics search engines value.

But link popularity is just one factor. And because search engine companies don't publicly reveal their algorithm's secret sauce, we listen to their advice on best practices.

But for everything else, it's mostly trial and error as we attempt to discern what other factors boost a site's ranking.

Consider that it's in the best interest of search providers to develop algorithms that deliver the most relevant information to their users.

This is no small task; it's estimated that there are over a billion websites on the Internet today.

The capacity to index all that data and serve it up intelligently and quickly is an expensive proposition. And while there are hundreds of search engines, Google and Bing garner roughly ninety-eight percent of all search traffic.

Ironically, the first major search engine, Yahoo, now uses Bing to provide its search results.

Now, let's look at a few ways to up your SEO game.

Begin with good design and content.

Are you sensing a theme?

The way in which a website is designed, from its navigation, usability, content, and accessibility all play a role in how well a site is ranked.

These factors provide an indirect, but measurable influence on a site's external popularity, which both Google and Bing interpret as a mark of a quality website.

Would you link to a crummy looking website? Probably not.

Moreover, advanced artificial intelligence now allows search engines the ability to accurately predict what humans would judge as a low or high-quality site.

While design matters, great content is the core of a quality website. Search engine users come with an intent to find useful content.

And search engines attempt to rank and place that content in their results pages the best way possible to satisfy that intent.

Get some links.

For a search engine to find and adequately catalog the pages on your website, there first must be a link to it from a site already in its database. So, the next time its "spiders" crawl that site, it will find the link to yours and add it accordingly.

There are a couple of methods for making this happen. Creating links back to your website through an established site like social media, guest blogging, and online press releases are popular methods.

But most experts recommend going straight to the source and submitting your sitemap to Google and Bing through their webmaster tools.

This not only all but guarantees your site gets added quickly, but it provides a direct link to your site's content without having to wait for search engine spiders to return and crawl your site.

That means that new content gets added to the databases of search engines much quicker.

Give each page some SEO love.

Keyword is perhaps the most misunderstood term in search engine parlance, but there's nothing magic or mystical about it.

Keywords are simply the words that you hope search users will use to find your website, product, or blog article.

At one time, bad actors used keywords nefariously by stuffing them into the keyword tags of websites to fool search engines into providing top rankings. Today's search engines completely ignore those tags.

But keyword usage is still part of any search engine's algorithm. And the best method to utilize keywords is to write good content that will be read and understood by humans. Most experts advise keyword usage of .5 to 2.5 percent of your page's content.

But beyond what your visitor sees on the page, there are a couple of areas outside the main content of a web page that deserve attention.

Meta tags, for example, are a type of web code that appears in the top section of each page.

At one time, it required some HTML knowledge to find and modify these tags.

Today, most modern web management systems are equipped to allow people with even minimal technical skills the ability to easily update their website's SEO information.

Let's look at the primary SEO page components with which you should be concerned.

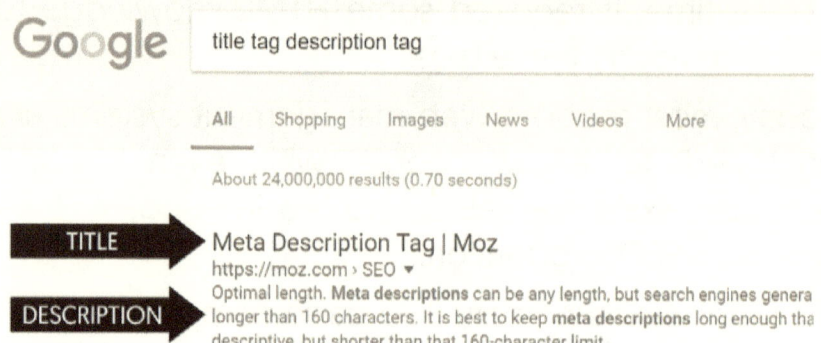

Title Tag

The information you enter in a title tag gets displayed as the page title on a search engine results page, which is the first item a search user will read. It needs to be descriptive, and if possible, include at least one or two keywords.

But keep it brief; most search engines allow only fifty-five characters, including spaces.

Description

Almost as important, the description displays under the title on the search results.

While it's good to have some keywords here, it's arguably more important to provide an accurate and compelling description of the page so that it encourages the search user to click through to your site.

Brevity is essential here as well.

You'll need to describe your page in less than 160 characters. Keep in mind that if your page description tag is empty, the search engine will display the first text it finds on the page.

And in many cases, that's not likely to be the ideal solution.

URLs

The web address, or URL, of each page of your site, also displays in the search results. And while it can impact the click-through rate, proper keyword usage is widely believed to affect rankings.

While there are no character limitations, it's good practice to keep URLs as short as possible and avoid spaces and non-characters, except hyphens.

Beyond the basics.

It's important to understand that this chapter covers just the basics of search engine optimization — and it's continually changing. Search engines are continually refining their algorithms to provide better results for their customers.

At one time, it was easy to fool search engines by merely manipulating the keywords meta tag or stuffing keywords onto pages in hyperlinks.

Today, variables such as intent and the geographic location of a user can vary the results between a person in California and that of someone in New York — even using identical keyword queries!

Moreover, all search traffic is not equal.

Your site could be getting a million visitors a day, but when that traffic doesn't convert into leads or sales, how valuable is it?

Getting the SEO basics right will put you light years ahead of the significant portion of website owners, many of which still have "Home" as the title tag for their home page.

Avoid the Pitfalls

CHAPTER FIVE

Not so long ago, Matthew Carpenter, a young Australian entrepreneur, launched an evil online business.

For a small fee, anyone could have an envelope filled with glitter delivered to a person they would likely never want to speak to again.

Like many budding business people, Carpenter put together a simple website to sell his service. And, like many aspiring business people, he didn't plan for success.

Ryan Hoover at the website, *Product Hunt* declared Carpenter's endeavor, ShipYourEnemiesGlitter.com, "The ultimate troll product," while Redditors were upvoting the site at a furious pace.

Shortly after launch, the site went viral, and the orders started pouring in.

But his website crashed, and his bargain-basement email storage limit was quickly exhausted, leaving him racing to delete unneeded emails while hundreds of new emails were hitting his inbox every hour.

And then there was the logistics of processing the orders — glitter, envelopes, ugh!

Clearly, Carpenter had not adequately thought through his business model.

But don't feel sorry for Carpenter. While he had a few trying days, he claims his revenue exceeded $20k before shuttering the website. And he sold the domain name for a whopping $85,000!

As I've said before, it's relatively simple to build a website today. But it's not so easy to create an **exceedingly good one** that fulfills its purpose and meets business goals.

And in this increasingly sophisticated digital age, an effective website is likely to be an essential key to the success of most businesses.

While there are many mistakes people make while developing a website — like poor navigation, too much clutter, or inconsistent branding — the most critical pitfalls may not be the most obvious.

Don't fall prey to scams.

Arguably, the domain name is the single point of failure for nearly every website. Lose control of your domain or let it expire — and no one will be able to find your site.

If you don't know where your domain name is registered, who has access to it, and the name of the registrant, I recommend taking action to find out today.

A domain review is one of the first exercises I go through with every new client, and I cannot emphasize enough the importance of domain name security.

Domain Name Scams

When you register a domain name, it's typically through what's called a registrar, like GoDaddy.

One of the quickest ways to lose your domain name is by falling prey to a scam called domain slamming, in which the offending domain name registrar attempts to trick domain owners into switching from their existing registrar to theirs, under the pretense that the customer is merely renewing their subscription to their current registrar.

Here's an example of a letter I've received many times:

> As a courtesy to domain name holders, we are sending you this notification for your business Domain name search engine registration. This letter is to inform you that it's time to send in your registration and save.
>
> Failure to complete your Domain name search engine registration by the expiration date may result in cancellation of this offer making it difficult for your customers to locate you on the web.

A legitimate domain registrar would never send a notice like this. In fact, most registrars use automated billing in which the default setting is to auto-renew each year. The only notification you would receive is if the credit card on file failed.

The easiest way to protect yourself from a domain name scam is knowledge: You know, or someone you trust knows, where and how your domain name is registered.

Your website provider should also be able to tell you where your domain name is registered and clarify if any notification you receive is legitimate.

Search Engine Scams

Another popular scam today is perpetrated by less-than-scrupulous organizations posing as Search Engine Optimization (SEO) companies who guarantee a number-one ranking on "all the search engines."

It's important to understand how disingenuous guarantees are with regards to search engine rankings.

Companies that provide legitimate search engine optimization consulting and development services rarely ever offer guarantees (and virtually never use it as a marketing tactic).

Why?

The search engines expressly warn against it. Visit the webmaster guidelines for Google or Bing, and you'll find they provide clear instructions on how to submit a site and what factors go into how that site is ranked.

There is no priority submission, no unique relationships, or special treatment for anyone.

No one can guarantee a #1 ranking on Google or Bing.

Reserve the same skepticism for unsolicited email about search engines as you do for "burn fat at night" diet pills or requests to help transfer funds from deposed dictators.

Additionally, search rankings are inherently unstable because so many dynamic variables are involved.

Say I perform a search for "SEO Company" in Washington, DC, then drive four hours south to Roanoke, Virginia and execute the same query. I'm likely to end up with a very different ordering of results or different results altogether.

A similar principle applies when I'm logged into my Google account where I get personalized results based on my search history.

Here's a snippet from an email that I've received before:

> I was reviewing your website and noticed that website has a good design and it looks good. But it was not ranked on GOOGLE for most of the keywords. I didn't find your website on the first page with your business keywords/ phrases. We can help you do better in all search engines by improving ranking. We are a leading search engine optimization service provider in your area. We also offer the most competitive rates for this service.

My site wasn't ranked for most of the keywords? Which keywords? How would they even know?

Here's another:

This email is being sent out to you because search registration for yourdomain.com is pending.

Please register these domains to search engines like Google, Bing and Yahoo ASAP to avoid late fees.

Registering for search engines would help you show up in search results and increase your online presence.

You can register your domain at link given below:

We sincerely appreciate your business! If you require anything, we are at your service.

Remember: If you do not register your domain with the search engines, it may not appear in the search engine listing when people are looking for you. Failure to complete your domain name search engine registration by the expiration date.

Roughly ninety-eight percent of all search traffic goes through Google and Bing. And listing a site with either search engine is a simple (and free) process.

But for many business owners, this is unknown territory filled with mystical words like meta tags, SERP, and keywords.

And unfortunately, they will gladly pay a fee to make sure their site appears in the search engine listings. But hiring a company that sends unsolicited emails is unlikely to accomplish this objective.

Choosing the wrong platform can cost you plenty.

When we discuss website platforms, we're mainly talking about the Content Management System or a CMS. Some CMS are built into the hosting application, which merely means the CMS cannot be separated from the hosting provider. This is true of many do-it-yourself services like Wix, Weebly, or Squarespace.

Selecting the proper platform for your business needs is vital to the long-term success of your website. Not all website platforms are the same, and there are hundreds from which to choose.

The primary consideration is that the CMS should fit the business objective of the website. For example, if your plan is to sell products online, you should use a CMS built for e-commerce — not a blogging CMS that's been modified for e-commerce.

Keep in mind that the choice of a CMS will likely determine the web development company — few companies are experts in more than a couple of CMS platforms.

For most small businesses, there are many good options. But for companies with large, content-rich websites, hiring a consultant for a business case analysis is money well-spent. Migrating site content from one system to another is always a tricky proposition and one that can get expensive in a hurry.

And this is where many business owners realize they've decided poorly — it's not typically evident early in the website's history, but when the business grows, and the site needs to scale accordingly.

Some considerations when evaluating a CMS:

- SEO technical issues like custom page URLs and image names

- Ability to export site content as a database

- Ability to update design/template

- Ability to control content on specific devices and screen resolutions

BTW - Most of these features are not available with many of the do-it-yourself services.

Unfriendly screen resolutions get no love.

A website that is not optimized for mobile devices such as smartphones and tablets is likely to have a detrimental effect on a business. Mobile traffic is increasing exponentially. Ignoring these devices puts a company at a competitive disadvantage.

Indeed, turning a blind eye to the proliferation of mobile devices can be detrimental to a site's search engine rankings. Both Google and Bing factor mobile-friendliness into search results.

"Starting April 21, 2015, we will be expanding our use of mobile-friendliness as a ranking signal."

~ Official Google News

How do you know if a website is mobile-friendly? Well, if you must pinch and zoom to read the site content easily, it's likely that site is not mobile-friendly.

There are a couple of ways to achieve a friendly screen resolution solution.

For existing sites, some services replicate your site's content and serve it up from their server when it detects a mobile device.

While there are several services available for websites of most any size, this should be considered a stop-gap or temporary solution.

Why? In most cases, a mobile version of your website means a copy of your site, which often means managing two sites. Moreover, there are possible search engine optimization ramifications.

The best practice for a mobile-friendly site is through a design process called responsive web design, which allows a website to adapt to different screen resolutions through a "fluid" design that either nudges content down on smaller screens, displays alternate content, or completely hides it.

And because most the screen sizes on most mobile devices are relatively standard, a designer can say, display navigation links as finger-friendly buttons on phone-sized screens.

Modern websites can vary significantly, but few details can have such an impact on the success of a site than falling prey to scams, choosing the wrong platform, and ignoring your mobile audience.

The Psychology of Choice

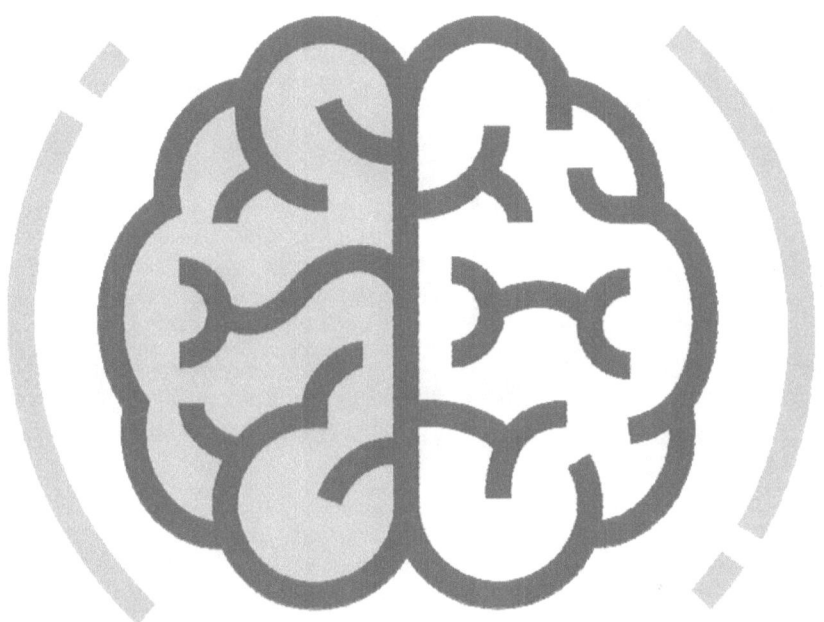

CHAPTER SIX

Every day, we make choices. From the clothes we wear to the food we eat.

But according to the behavioral economist, Dan Ariely, many of those decisions may not reside within our choosing.

People like choices, but give them too many options, or decisions that may be difficult, and they are likely to freeze.

And in many cases, a person faced with a difficult decision may gravitate to whatever has been chosen for them.

To illustrate this point, Ariely uses the example of European organ donor participation rates. Of the eleven countries that include organ donor registration at the Department of Motor Vehicles, participation rates in four of those countries reached only as high as twenty-eight percent (and that was after the Netherlands conducted an exhaustive enrollment campaign).

But in the other seven countries, participation rates reached one-hundred percent, with one exception at eighty-six percent. Oddly enough, there seemed to be no identifiable cause from any of the usual factors like culture, geography, ethnicity, race, or gender.

What caused such a discrepancy?

It turns out the determining factor was the form used at the DMV. The countries with low participation rates were using an opt-in question requiring people to check the box if they **wanted to participate** in the organ donor program. And what happened? People didn't check the box, and they didn't join.

The countries with the high participation rates had a slightly different form — one with an opt-out question — that required people to check the box if they **didn't want** to participate. Interestingly, people didn't check the box. But in this scenario, by default, they joined the donor program.

"It's not because we don't care," Ariely says. *"It's the opposite. It's because we care. It's difficult and it's complex. And it's so complex that we don't know what to do. And because we have no idea what to do, we just pick whatever it was that was chosen for us."*

What Ariely is talking about here is what is referred to as cognitive dissonance — or overload. For website owners, this means that often the easiest way to get someone to take the desired action is to present them with a default choice.

Think about the last time you encountered a website homepage cluttered with too much information: Did it made your head spin?

That uncomfortable feeling is dissonance and what often results in that scenario is the visitor navigating away to another website.

Sites with a high bounce rate (when a visitor leaves a site without clicking any links), can usually be traced back to either unclear information, cluttered, or too much information.

If you're like me, you probably receive more than one or two email subscriptions. Think about the newsletters that you read regularly. It's likely that those emails are simple in design, single-column, with clear and concise language.

But dissonance can also occur when we are presented with **too many** choices.

Dr. Sheena Iyengar, the author of "The Art of Choosing," conducted a study on this subject while she was a doctoral student at Stanford. Her somewhat-famous "jam" study involved research assistants setting out jars of jam on tables in a supermarket and offering samples to shoppers.

One table had six jars while the other had twenty-four. While the latter attracted more visitors, the former had a higher percentage of sales. The six-jar table converted thirty percent of visitors into customers while just three percent of the visitors to the twenty-four-jar table purchased jam.

Choice overload can have consequential effects when we choose not to decide, even when it's in our best interests.

In her TED talk, "On the Art of Choosing," Iyengar gives an example of a study in which she evaluated the retirement savings decisions of nearly a million Americans.

She wanted to understand whether the number of fund offerings available in a retirement savings plan affected a person's likelihood to save more.

What she found was that there was in fact, a correlation. The more funds offered, the lower the participation rate.

Let's look at a few examples of how we can apply these principles to your marketing efforts.

Creating quality landing pages.

"One Page. One Purpose. Period."

That's the advice from Oli Gardner of *Unbounce*, a landing page and conversion marketing company.

The most common purposes of a landing page are to generate leads or sales. Either way, the singular goal of that landing page is getting the visitor to fill out the form or make a purchase — conversion.

Remove anything that distracts from that goal.

A good landing page should have no site navigation or external links. It should have a clear headline, message, and call-to-action.

Shopify's trial landing page nails it on nearly every point.

It's simple, clear, provides social proof, and requires just an email address to get started.

Website product/service pricing.

Many startups spend a lot of effort and money driving traffic to their websites only to neglect one of the most important pages — the pricing page!

This is one area in which the psychology of choice can have the most impact on a business. While there's not a one-size-fits-all solution, there are some basic best practices you can employ to maximize conversions and profits.

The most popular method is to highlight a single option. You'll see this technique used on many websites today.

The example below from *Highrise* follows a common practice of three choices but also uses language (most popular plan), that makes it easy for a visitor to choose. Note that it's not the most expensive plan either.

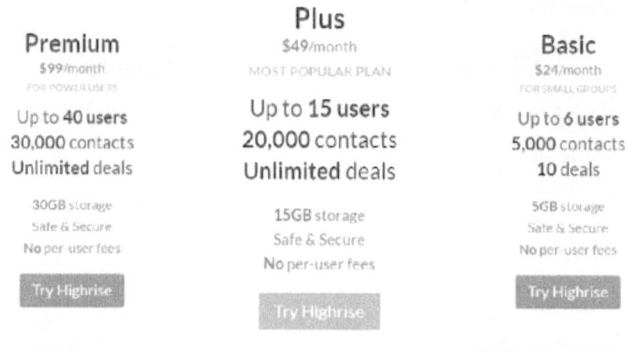

30-day Free Trial on All Accounts

Pick a plan & sign up in 60 seconds. Upgrade, downgrade, cancel at any time.

Plus
$49/month
MOST POPULAR PLAN

Premium
$99/month
FOR POWER USERS

Basic
$24/month
FOR SMALL GROUPS

Up to **15 users**
20,000 contacts
Unlimited deals

Up to **40 users**
30,000 contacts
Unlimited deals

Up to **6 users**
5,000 contacts
10 deals

15GB storage
Safe & Secure
No per-user fees

30GB storage
Safe & Secure
No per-user fees

5GB storage
Safe & Secure
No per-user fees

Try Highrise

Try Highrise

Try Highrise

30-day free trial on all accounts

We also offer a solo plan (1 user, 5 GB file storage, unlimited deals, 20k contacts, $29/month)

Everything in your Highrise account is safe, secure, and password-protected.

Purposeful email marketing.

Like landing pages, email marketing should be singularly focused while fulfilling your promise to your subscribers (why they signed up).

Emails should compel subscribers to act by providing a sense of urgency and a clear call-to-action.

Here's where the button language can help drive engagement. Make sure to use language that is specific but inviting.

Friction words like submit, order, buy, or download implies effort. By focusing on the benefit and using words like "get" or "learn," you're likely to increase clicks.

Some marketers choose to add links like website navigation, but I'm a big fan of keeping links to a minimum with the focus on the call-to-action buttons.

The invitation below for SXSW is an excellent example of singularly-focused email marketing with a single call-to-action.

There are many other great examples of how brands are implementing choice psychology in their marketing. But don't just copy what others are doing. You should be testing your marketing by collecting data that's uniquely your own.

Determine your strategy based on your business model, but test colors, fonts, pricing models, and the number of plans you offer. Test everything. What works for another business may or may not work for yours.

Context and options can drastically influence the outcome of a decision — whether it's a buying decision, opting into a newsletter, or participating in an organ donor program.

Limiting the number of options presented to a consumer doesn't necessarily mean reducing the number of products or services. Rather, presenting them wisely; like limiting the number of items per row, with large, clear descriptions.

Applying these principles of psychology to your website and daily marketing routines can be powerful for any business.

Do-It-Yourself Tools

CHAPTER SEVEN

You can do-it-yourself.

Should you?

In recent years, the rise of online tools has democratized the web in ways that enable business owners to publish websites, landing pages, and other digital marketing assets quickly and efficiently.

What once was the sole domain of the IT department, is now readily available to non-techies everywhere.

Online website builders have lowered the barrier to entry as well.

What once would cost thousands of dollars and months to complete can now be live in a few hours and for just a few dollars a month.

Like most things in life, online website building tools have their pros and cons — just because you can, doesn't necessarily mean you should.

First, a look at the cons of doing it yourself.

The cost will always be a primary consideration for many new businesses. Unfortunately, the real costs of DIY website development are not always present and upfront.

Most popular online website builders use a freemium model, which is to say that in many cases, it costs nothing to create an account and "build" your website. That is until you assign your domain to it, want an email address (@yourdomain.com), or add most any basic functionality features like a contact form.

Need support? That's likely going to cost extra as well.

But the most significant cost for your new free website is often not calculated into the equation: Your time.

Indeed, these online website tools are just that — tools. Some are relatively easy to understand, but others — especially the more feature-rich versions — include a steep learning curve.

It's not uncommon for novices to spend months getting their website to match their vision. It's also not unusual that many people leave frustrated and hire a professional company to either fix their problems or start over entirely.

It's not all bad.

Several online tools have been around for years, are clear about their pricing, and have thousands of satisfied customers.

In many cases, it comes down to the purpose of the website.

For creative types like artists and photographers, Squarespace shines. Most of their templates are designed for portfolio-type websites and are well-designed.

Need a space to showcase your writing? WordPress.com is an excellent choice with hundreds of ready-to-go blogging templates available.

And WordPress is specially designed for blogging, making it easy to copy from a Word or Google document and paste directly into their online editor, with little formatting cleanup.

A suitable online website builder is likely to cost somewhere between $10 - $30 a month. Not bad for something that would cost thousands more if it were developed from scratch.

But there are some caveats.

It's essential to understand the potential pitfalls of online website builders fully.

In most cases, you'll be using a template as your jumping off point, and there will be limitations to how much the design can be changed. Moreover, many of these themes require a lot of photography to look good, so you'll need to have access to quality image assets.

Make no mistake: the best-looking examples in the showcases of these companies were developed by seasoned professionals, experienced in working with that specific platform.

Possibly the most problematic issue is the one of content ownership.

You spend countless days (and possibly nights) working on your website, tweaking this, adjusting that, adding content, and writing articles, only to login in one day and find that all of it is gone. Not just unavailable but gone.

The terms of service for many website builders outline that they have the right to determine the ownership of "User Content." Yep, that means, in many cases, you don't own or control your content.

You know all those times you just check the box to agree to the terms of service when signing up for an account? This is one where you should really take the time to read the terms of service.

And other than WordPress, most website builders do not function from data-driven content management systems, which is to say each page you create stands alone instead of being stored in a database.

The importance of this feature lies in the ability to easily backup or export your site's content.

With static sites, the only way to move your site's content would be manually. Think: copy, paste, repeat.

While that may not be too bad for small sites, migrating content-rich websites, especially those with extensive image assets, is likely to be as much fun as a root canal.

Search engine optimization tools?

At one time, online website builders like Wix, Weebly, and Squarespace were so horribly built, it was nearly impossible for search engines to find your website and its content.

That's changed in recent months, and all those services now feature the ability to customize your URL, add alt tags [text descriptions] to images, and create custom page titles and descriptions.

Search the review sites, and you'll likely find a lot of complaints about the lack of SEO tools, but most pre-date the software upgrades.

While Wix, Weebly, and SquareSpace seem to have this critical piece figured out, many still do not.

Website builders can be an excellent tool for someone with a marketing background and a little web knowledge who needs to get a website off the ground quickly.

And there are several excellent options available for doing just that. There are also a ton of terrible tools out there as well.

There are many potential downsides with the do-it-yourself route.

Choosing the right tool for the type of website you're building is an important decision that should be made after considerable due diligence.

Caveat emptor.

Making Sure Your Website is Social Media-Ready

CHAPTER EIGHT

Why it's important.

Unless you landed on this planet yesterday, it's highly likely you have read or posted an article someone else shared on Facebook or Twitter. Okay, so maybe "read" is a little assumptive.

It's also likely you've never wondered how it works — how the information appears, and in what section of the post. Or how Facebook's software determines what image to display, and what size works best.

There's nothing magical to it. But if you own or run a website, it's important to understand how it all works because you want to make it easy for people to share your website's content — and for that content to look professional across all platforms.

When a website page is shared on Facebook or Twitter, the app is looking for some specific code called "meta tags." Absent these tags, it's likely the first image on the page will appear along with a snippet from the first paragraph of text, which may be less than ideal.

Worse, without this code, Twitter will only display the web address.

It seems that this is one of the areas of website development most overlooked by designers, which is sad given how simple an element it is to include.

Indeed, having the proper meta tags implemented can affect click-through and conversion rates, so the return on this small investment can be significant given social media's ever-increasing role in digital marketing.

In most of this book, I refrain from using technical jargon or providing detailed instructions for fear of losing the reader — you.

This is the only chapter I include technical information for purely reference. Most readers will likely not need the information on pages 101-105 other than to give to a website manager or developer.

Let's first look at how it all works; then we'll dive into implementation.

Facebook and their Open Graph tags.

In 2010, Facebook introduced a protocol for meta tags which has become the standard for how information travels from a website to social media when a page is shared.

By efficiently using Open Graph tags, of which there are several, you can control what information appears in the post's title, description, and what image(s) will be displayed.

This is not dissimilar from meta tags used for controlling what content gets displayed on search engine results pages.

While there are several types of Open Graph tags, for this chapter, we'll focus on just the image, title, and description — the three tags relevant to shared content.

OG Image →

OG Title →
OG Description →

In the example above, we can see the article has been optimized for Facebook using Open Graph (OG) tags.

There's limited real estate for each area, so it's important to make sure your title doesn't exceed 90 characters, and the description is less than 250 characters (150 for mobile devices). Otherwise, Facebook will truncate it with a trailing ellipsis.

Before publication, it's always a good idea to make sure everything looks as intended. We always run new posts through Facebook's Sharing Debugger, which will display a preview of how the post will look when it's shared. It will also provide feedback on any problems it detects.

Additionally, the debugger tool allows you to clear Facebook's page cache, which is especially important if you make a change to a page after it's been shared.

Keep in mind that unless you clear the cache, Facebook will continue to display the old information each time the shared page is displayed in the news feed.

A word about LinkedIn.

LinkedIn also follows the Open Graph protocol, so many of the same rules apply. It will display your title and image in much the same way Facebook does.

However, it doesn't seem to display the description. I've tested this on LinkedIn's website and through the app. No matter what page I've used (with adequately defined Open Graph tags), it displays just the title and the image.

Twitter has Cards.

With the introduction of Cards in 2013, Twitter jazzed up their boring text-only posts and whether intentional or not, moved toward looking more like Facebook. Cards allow content developers to display an image, title, and description when their content is shared on Twitter instead of just a page URL.

As you can see from the example above, the Card-optimized Tweet is displayed much like a Facebook post.

Yes, there's more to Cards than just emulating a Facebook post, but for the sake of brevity and consistency, we'll stick to only these three elements.

Making the magic happen on your website.

Implementation of Open Graph and Twitter Cards is a simple process. Depending on how your site was developed will determine the type of implementation that will work best.

As many of today's websites are built on WordPress, we'll start there.

Of course, you'll need a plugin, and there are more than a few options. You can go with the official Facebook plugin, which has a lot of nice features, but I recommend *Yoast SEO*. It's a freemium plugin with a lot of extra features not found in the Facebook plugin.

First, it allows for Search Engine Optimization (SEO) as well as Open Graph and Twitter Cards. Additionally, it provides XML sitemaps, page analysis, and an easy way of controlling which pages Google shows in its search results and which pages it doesn't show.

Once you have the plugin installed, the instructions for enabling Open Graph and Twitter cards is straightforward.

If your website requires a developer to customize your site for Open Graph and Twitter Cards, they'll need a few lines of markup to place in the top section of the page template for each article pages.

For Open Graph:

```
<meta property="og:title" content="Your Awesome
Article Title"/>

<meta property="og:description" content="This awesome
article is really awesome."/>

<meta property="og:url"
content="https://yourwebsite.com/your-awesome-
article"/>

<meta property="og:image"
content="https://yourwebsite.com/article-image.jpg">
```

For Twitter Cards:

```
<meta name="twitter:card"
content="summary_large_image">

<meta name="twitter:title" content="Your Awesome
Article Title"/>

<meta name="twitter:description" content="This awesome
article is really awesome."/>

<meta name="twitter:url"
content="https://yourwebsite.com/your-awesome-
article"/>

<meta name="twitter:image"
content="https://yourwebsite.com/article-image.jpg">
```

As you can see, the only real difference is that Twitter *requires* the `twitter:card` tag to identify the type of Card. In our example code, we are defining a Card with a large image. Other options include a small image or a carousel of images.

And like Facebook, Twitter has a debugger of sorts. They call it a validator, and it can be persnickety. I've found that often it can take multiple attempts before you get a valid response.

Also, you'll need to ensure that Twitter's bot is allowed to crawl your image directory. Otherwise, your Twitter image will not get displayed.

Keep in mind that if your pages have been tweeted previously, you'll need to validate *each* URL to clear Twitter's cache.

A couple of tips to keep in mind.

It's worth noting that Twitter Cards will fall back to defined Open Graph tags for the URL, title, description, and image if the Cards markup for those elements is not present. But remember the `twitter:card` tag must be present and defined.

However, the image size requirements for Twitter and Facebook vary slightly and can influence how or if the image gets displayed. For best results, both channels recommend an image with roughly a 2:1 ratio. The same applies for LinkedIn.

With that said, images must meet a minimum size to be displayed. For Twitter, images must be a minimum dimension of 300x157 or maximum of 4096x4096 pixels and must be less than 5MB in size.

Facebook recommends images that are at least 1200 x 630 pixels for the best display on high-resolution devices. At the minimum, you should use images that are 600 x 315 pixels to display link page posts with larger images.

Facebook images can be up to 8MB in size, but I can't think of a scenario in which you would ever want to use a file that large.

Additionally, the maximum character length for Facebook and Twitter vary. While your Facebook title can be up to 150 characters, Twitter limits it to just 70.

And the description can be no longer than 124 characters compared to 150 for Facebook. For this reason, it's best practice to create a separate title and description for Twitter Cards.

There's much more that can be done with Open Graph and Cards than mentioned here but getting the basics in place will go a long way to helping your content stand out and increase engagement.

Hiring the Right Team

CHAPTER NINE

Beginning the selection process.

Ask any experienced business owner how the development of their website went and you'll likely to get an angry look or a reply something like, "which version?"

Venturing into your first website project can be a frustrating proposition without giving proper due diligence to the selection of a web development company. And it's one that can have long-lasting ramifications.

Throughout my career in web development, I've seen (or heard about) the good, the bad, and the ugly. What I can tell you for sure is that the value of an experienced consultant cannot be understated.

Googling "web design" can carry you only so far.

What follows are five of the most important factors to consider when choosing a web development company.

Determine what type of website you need.

That may sound like a given, but not all websites are the same.

Google is a website. But it's powered by a multibillion-dollar infrastructure with several data centers around the globe.

Facebook and Amazon? Ditto.

While those may be extreme examples, it's crucial to distinguish differences in what makes up a website and its functionality, which is to say what you need the site to do for your visitors and your business.

Are you going to sell widgets? Well, you're going to need an e-commerce website, and it's unlikely your buddy's cousin is going to be well-suited for this project.

Why? E-commerce brings with it several logistical and technological challenges. The company you hire should have experience working in the e-commerce space, and have an e-commerce solution that will scale with the growth of your business — and provide support for the inevitable glitches that occur along the way.

For many small businesses offering professional services, the primary objectives of a website are to build trust, educate, inform, and convert visitors into leads.

While there are hundreds of web development companies that can handily accomplish this task, there are several variables to consider, such as what type of content management system will be used and where the site will be hosted.

These factors can have a significant impact on the website's daily management and down the road when, not if, the site is redesigned.

Determine your compatibility.

When you hire a web development company, you are hiring a technology partner. This partner will likely be part of your business for many years, given you are happy with their service.

And that's the rub.

Spending a little extra time on the front side can save your business a lot of money and more importantly, a lot of time.

Moving a website from one provider to another can be costly and time-consuming.

Get to know who you are hiring for this long-term relationship. While the quality and efficacy of their work is undoubtedly a consideration, find out what they value, how they work, and how they treat their staff.

And while credibility and trust are also important traits, it's also nice if you like them.

Determine the level of support you need.

Support comes in several forms, like help with setting up email or helping someone reset a password.

With website support, you'll likely need changes to your site on a regular basis. It's not uncommon to realize a feature or element was left unconsidered before launch.

And more importantly, a website is not, nor should be static.

A good development company is going to provide you with the tools to add and update content, add new pages and articles, and make minor updates.

For new features, it's likely you'll need to rely on your technology partner.

Most web development companies provide some level of on-going support, but it's always a good idea to find out what level, turnaround time, and which members of the staff will be doing this type of work.

Attention to details?

Recently, someone in my network announced the launch of their new website. I could tell from their post they were excited and proud of their new online presence. Of course, there was a link to the new site in the post. But it displayed nothing but the logo and the title from the home page, "Home."

Epic fail.

The launch of a new site is an opportunity to shine on social media. But because their web developer either didn't take the time or perhaps didn't understand how social media channels work, the opportunity was lost. More importantly, the lack of the proper title and description will likely harm their search engine rankings.

It's small details like this that, over time, can help make or break a brand's digital properties. A good web development company has the experience and understands the importance of how social media and search engines display information from websites. They work with your company to make sure these bases are covered so that you'll always be putting your best face forward.

And it shows attention to detail — the kind of company who ensures that everything is checked, then double-checked.

Factor in all the costs.

Website design and development pricing run the gamut from free, to fixed, to hourly. Heck, some companies even have tiered pricing based on the type of person do the work.

Beyond the initial design and development costs, there will be on-going charges should be understood before signing the contract.

Hosting

Nearly every web development company charges something for hosting a website, but even this can vary widely. While it might be tempting, this is the area in which you don't want to be chintzy. In most cases, you get what you pay for, and that means site uptime — you want your site to be available all the time, not just some of the time. Don't skimp on costs here.

On-Going Support

Again, this is an area where pricing is all over the board. Some companies include a certain level of support in their hosting plans, while other charge time and materials for any change. It's important to understand that you *will* make changes to your website and there is likely to be a cost. It's better to understand and plan for those costs on the front side.

There's no definitive guide for web development, and every company operates with differing business models, so there's no silver bullet for finding the right website development team.

But with a little homework on the front side, you can hopefully mitigate some of the costs of building, maintaining, and (eventually) rebuilding your website.

Who Owns Your Website?

CHAPTER TEN

"For every complex problem, there is an answer that is clear, simple, and wrong."

H.L. Menken's observation might as well have been a prognostication of today's digital age.

The hand-held computers we call phones — which provide us access to a wealth of entertainment and knowledge Menken's generation couldn't have imagined — are the epitome of the complex made simple.

And all of it just works.

Install a new app, and it configures itself with little assistance or guidance.

If you've had a website built recently, the chances are good that it too, just works. A far cry from what web development looked like just a decade ago.

But beneath that façade of simplicity lies several layers of complexities. And determining what, if any part of your website you in fact own can be tricky to say with any degree of certainty.

Let's begin with the parts you don't own.

You don't own your domain name.

Each website is comprised of several assembled parts, the first and arguably the most important, is the domain name.

It's important to understand that domain name registration doesn't confer any legal ownership of the domain name, just an exclusive right to use it for a specified time.

While it's true one can sell the rights to the domain, it's not true ownership but more of a contract like what you have with your wireless carrier for your mobile number.

Even still, you should make sure that no matter who registers your domain, they register it in your name. And, as I mentioned previously, avoid making the all too common mistake of filing away the registration credentials in a place where it will be forgotten or misplaced.

Remember, if your domain name fails to get renewed each year, your visitors will not find your website.

You don't typically own the code.

Because the front-end source code used to create modern websites often originates from a templating framework like *Foundation* or *Bootstrap*, it's owned by the respective creators.

The only way you would own the source code is if you or your employee authors it from scratch — otherwise it's owned by the creator and licensed to you.

That line of thinking also applies to the web server platform, programming code, database software, and CMS (Content Management System) on which your website runs.

It's unlikely you own your server.

Modern website hosting typically involves more than one server. Alternatively, a low-cost provider will host multiple websites (sometimes into the thousands) on a single server.

In most cases, you lease space from a service provider to host a website.

Technically, you could purchase a server and create your own data center, but it's not the smartest way to spend your money.

You should own your website content.

The text, the visual design, and all the imagery that make up your website's content should be yours. But even here, there can be some uncertainty.

You would own the entirety of your website content if you or your employee created it. But because few companies develop their website in-house, it's important to read and fully understand the contract you might have with a development company.

Surprisingly, the contracts employed by many web design firms give them the legal ownership of the content they develop. And it's usually only when a business decides to migrate their site to another provider do they find out the bad news.

Additionally, it's common practice for many companies to license stock photography for use in the websites they develop for their clients, meaning the development company owns the license, not you.

Again, if you or one of your employees took the picture, you own it.

Cover your bases and avoid becoming a hostage.

Unfortunately, there are bad people in the world.

But understanding what pieces of your website you own and what should be in your control goes a long way to avoiding trouble.

And as I've said before, when you hire a web development company, you're creating a partnership that will likely last for years.

It's not always apparent what problems a lousy partnership might create, but it's easy to become hostage to a web development company or a "web guy" without proper due diligence on the front side.

While development contracts that place restrictions on creative ownership get a lot of attention, the most common problem situation is one in which the web development company registered your domain — in their name or with an account other than yours.

While this is, in many cases, expedient, it gives them full control over your website.

Recently, an opportunist attempted to take advantage of a Phoenix-based company who misplaced their domain registration credentials.

When the company representative asked for the account information, Tavis Tso, their IT professional, told them he didn't have it, redirected the company's website to a blank page, and disabled the company's email accounts.

Then, he offered to "fix" the problem for the low price of $10,000. When the company refused his offer, he redirected the company's domain to a porn site.

Tso was eventually convicted of Computer Fraud, but not before causing some serious headaches.

The legalities of owning a website can often be unclear, but not impossible to determine.

Beginning the website development process with a trusted partner who provides a clear understanding of all the elements involved will go a long way towards protecting your investment and your sanity.

Conclusion

Solving your puzzle.

Each website project in which I've participated has been about solving a problem.

For many businesses, employing a website is an attempt to solve a similar problem: Driving engagement, and in turn, driving sales.

With every problem, there are a multitude of possible solutions.

Many have already been solved.

The answers are out there but are rarely found in one place with a cute, neat bow tied around them.

This purpose of this book is to provide many of the answers to the website development questions that businesses owners may not even know they should be asking.

Technology will continue to evolve, and design techniques will come and go. Who knows what the future holds?

But if businesses continue using websites for marketing their wares, it's unlikely that a well-planned site created with great content and a user-centered design will miss its mark.

Thanks for reading.

I hope this book provides the insight and information to help you manage your next website project smoothly, lower its costs, and save you time — and headaches.

If so, drop a line to jclark@diginovas.com and let me know how it's going.

I look forward to hearing from you.

Resources

Stuff we like and use.

At Diginovas, we have a toolbox of resources we use on a regular basis to develop websites.

I'm confident you'll find something useful here.

Search Engine Optimization

In the chapter on getting your site found, I discuss how easy it is to get your site listed. And it's free!

Here's where to start to get your site properly indexed by Google and Bing, which account for approximately ninety-eight percent of search traffic.

Google:

https://www.google.com/webmasters/tools/

Bing:

https://www.bing.com/webmaster/home/

There are a few tools online that allow you to test a site's page title tags and description. We use the tool from *To The Web*. The not-so short link is below.

https://totheweb.com/learning_center/tool-test-google-title-meta-description-lengths

For a more in-depth dive down the rabbit hole that is SEO, you should check out *The Beginners Guide to SEO* by MOZ.

https://moz.com/beginners-guide-to-seo

Image Assets

One of the most important assets an effective website employs is quality images.

There are roughly 3,000,000 websites that offer royalty-free stock images, but we typically use just a few resources.

Adobe Stock is our go-to for most business-related imagery. Their library is robust, and their site has easy-to-use filters to help you find the perfect image for the job.

At the time of this writing, their subscription plan provided ten standard assets a month for $29.99 — one of the best deals on the web for images of this quality.

https://stock.adobe.com

FreePhotos.cc and **Pexels.com** are free resources that curate creative commons-licensed photos from various websites. Each pulls from similar stock photo sites, but the search filters vary in helping find suitable images.

While not every image is especially useful for business websites, the quality is exceptional.

https://freephotos.cc

https://www.pexels.com

Social Media

Content marketing is typically a big part of any website's marketing and governance plan. Sharing that content through social media channels can be time-consuming without the proper tools.

And there are many tools available!

We have found **Buffer** easy to use and reasonably priced. At the time of this writing, they offered a free plan (with limited capabilities), a $10 a month plan, and a business plan (for teams and agencies) that started at $99 a month.

https://buffer.com

Email Marketing

Dollar for dollar, email marketing remains the best marketing value. But there are many moving parts, and it's often difficult for novices.

MailChimp does a good job of simplifying the process with beautiful templates (that work well in most email clients), an easy-to-use interface, and a free plan that fits well into the marketing strategy of many small businesses.

https://mailchimp.com

For a little more robust platform, **Campaign Monitor** is an exceptional tool. It's designed for agencies but works great for a small marketing team and has plenty of integration points with popular Customer Relationship Management (CRM) tools.

https://www.campaignmonitor.com

The Author

Jonathan Clark is the Founder and CEO of Diginovas, a company that specializes in website development for small businesses and startups.

As a successful business manager and owner, Jonathan is intimate with the challenges of running a business.

In 2002, he launched a web design company that, after five consecutive years of growth, was acquired in 2007.

For the next six years, he led the marketing efforts of a fast-growing software and web development company, creating and defining an identity that helped increase annual revenues and earn recognition for growth in Inc. and Florida Trend magazines.

Acknowledgements

Very special thanks go to my wife Kim, for once again filling the role as my editor. Her loving admonishments and advice have enhanced my writing skills immensely and greatly improved the readability of this book. I love you.